THE MILLER'S TALE
and Other Parables

Also by Margaret Silf

LANDMARKS: An Ignatian Journey

TASTE AND SEE: Adventuring into Prayer

DAYSPRINGS: Daily Readings for a Life with God

THE MILLER'S TALE

and Other Parables

MARGARET SILF

with illustrations by
ROY LOVATT

DARTON · LONGMAN + TODD

This collection first published in 2000 by
Darton, Longman and Todd Ltd
1 Spencer Court
140–142 Wandsworth High Street
London SW18 4JJ

The Miller's Tale was first published in 1996 by Avon Books.
Parts of 'The Thorn Bush' (in *The Wisdom of the Woods*) first appeared
in the journal *Spirituality* (Dominican Publications).

ISBN 0–232–52390–8

A catalogue record for this book is available from the British Library.

Designed and produced by Sandie Boccacci
using QuarkXPress on an Apple PowerMac 7500
Set in 10.5/13.25pt Bembo
Printed and bound in Great Britain by
Page Bros, Norwich, Norfolk

AD
MAJOREM
DEI
GLORIAM

CONTENTS

ᘏoᘒ

INTRODUCTION

❧

THE WORD OF GOD in sacred scripture has two sisters – an older sister and a younger sister.

The older sister is older than the hills. She is the created world in which we live and move and have our being.

The younger sister is as young as this morning. She is our own personal, everyday experience of life as we are living it in the here and now.

This collection of parables draws these three siblings together, in the belief that every stone has a story to tell, and every event and incident in our daily lives has the potential to disclose something of God and God's Kingdom.

These reflections trace a story from original blessing, through brokenness and restoration, to a vision of a new and never-ending Kingdom in which we are called to be active co-creators.

In 'The Miller's Tale', a fallen crab-apple tree and a restored waterwheel retell this story within the small green space of a mill garden.

A chance remark by an over-tired priest opens up, in 'The Necessary Rice', some of the scenarios of human sin and compulsion from which we long to be released.

In the end, all we can change is ourselves, and our own perceptions. 'Conversations with a Pumpkin' explores what it can mean, and what it can cost, to let go of the protective shell of our ego-selves to make way for Cinderella's coach of transformation.

The coach of transformation takes us to the Kingdom Ball, but we discover that the Kingdom is all-inclusive, and can never be merely an individual matter. 'Pan Piper' draws our gaze to the needs of those around us, and reveals Christ as the in-gatherer of the lost, healer of the broken, and inspirer of the despairing. A Christ who today (in the words of Teresa of Avila) has no eyes, no ears, no hands, no feet, but ours.

The life of all creation has something to reveal of the Creator's wisdom, but the contribution of any creature to the story of the Word can ever only be a partial one, a fragment of the whole. A tiny goldcrest leads us through 'The Wisdom of the Woods', and confounds our expectations in her choice of the 'king of the forest'.

The salvation story reaches its terrible crescendo in 'Night Crossing', but its meaning cannot be destroyed. The sea yields up its treasure and as the moonlight dips among the storm-waves so 'Christ plays in ten thousand places, lovely in limbs, and lovely in eyes not His' (Gerard Manley Hopkins).

'Crossroads' brings us to new beginnings, empowered by the constant presence of the risen Lord, to bring hope where there is despair, and life where there is death. The younger sister of the Word is commissioned for her own task of making the Gospel incarnate in the here and now.

May she lead us to the place where our prayer becomes wholly in-woven into our lives, and where the contemplation in the silence of our hearts is expressed as action in the tumult of our world.

~∘~

I would like to express my warmest gratitude to Katie Worrall, Helen Porter, Hannah Ward and all colleagues at Darton, Longman and Todd, who have brought this book into being, to Roy Lovatt for his inspirational illustrations, and to those fellow pilgrims whose friendship, wisdom and encouragement is a bedrock of faith and joy in my life.

THE
MILLER'S TALE

I T MUST BE WELL OVER FIVE YEARS since we were last here
at the old mill. It has changed hands since then. The new
miller and his wife came out to greet us, surprised that there
should be any visitors at all on this cold, windy, wintry April day.

It's a place of memory for me. Being here again, so un-
expectedly, evoked those memories, going back through the
years of our daughter's childhood, when we would occasionally,
as a special treat, get on the narrow-gauge steam railway down
the valley and come to the mill by train, breathing in all the
nostalgia of the smell of the steam and letting its power carry us
through this gentle landscape on the edge of the mountains and
the lakes.

Today it was so bleak – not like those distant summers when
the sun had always seemed to be shining on our little outings.
Today the fierce wind had driven us down from the mountains
and we had found ourselves at the mill more by accident than by
choice. In fact it was hard not to hurry the tour through the
chilly mill to get back to the warmth of the car, and hard to listen
attentively to the miller's commentary above the chattering of
our teeth. I had the sense of something lost along the path of
time, but the lost treasure was like a seed, fallen by the wayside,
that might spring to life again, if only the sun would shine.

It wasn't until I was sitting reflectively in front of a dying fire,
well past midnight, in the deep silence of a household where all
were sleeping except me, and where the only sound was the
crackling of the fire embers and the whistling of the wind in
the chimney and the steady rhythm of my own breathing – it
wasn't until that reflective hour that the images of the mill came
hurtling back to me, like excited children clamouring for my
attention, which I gave, gladly and eagerly.

I had just been reading about the opening of a new
monastery on the northern edge of London that was to be a
place of quiet retreat and meditative reflection for all who

might come to draw upon it. The monks had chosen to adopt the intertwined symbols of water, sun, a tree and an ear of wheat as their logo.

I suppose I must have taken these symbols subconsciously into my night prayer. For an hour or so I was simply at peace with myself and with God and with the fading firelight, not thinking, not feeling, not being anything except a breathing, living being, held in being by the source of all being. Perhaps it was prayer. Perhaps it verged on drowsy sleep.

Eventually I opened my eyes and suddenly, without warning, my imagination leapt to life, and I was standing beside the mill-race again, and asking myself, incredulously, how I could have been sitting here in front of the fire for a whole hour without making the obvious connection between what I had read this evening and what I had experienced this afternoon.

There was a memory of warm summer days when the sun shone generously on this grassy hillside place. There was the flow of the mill-race and the calm of the millpond, sparkling gently in the sunlight or hurling its waters recklessly into the waterwheel. There was an ancient crab-apple tree – how many generations of millers' families has it shaded, and tempted with its autumn fruits? And there was a sack of wheat, that I could run my fingers through and feel the tingle of the waiting grains, before they were surrendered to the ruthless rotation of the millstones.

Sun. Water. A tree. And wheat. And for me, two other elements besides: the cold, hard, reliable stone for the grinding, and the evocative, ephemeral cloud of steam from the engine that had brought us here and had perhaps, once, more usefully, brought the wheat for the grinding. In that mill-pasture, remembered in prayer, I discovered a story that is at once both my own story and the universal story. If you have time to linger for an hour beside the fires of your own imagination, we might walk a while together in the sun's warmth, by the mill-race, in the shade of the crab-apple tree, rubbing a grain of wheat between our fingers . . .

The Song of the Sun

Out of nowhere, beyond your horizon, beyond your understanding, I rose to make all things visible. You greeted my rising, you unformed earth. You warmed to my touch and brought forth all the creatures contained within your hidden, secret seeds. And the earth teemed. And I rose, higher, until all the earth was alight and alive.

Out of the embers of past generations, I raised up in you a new day. You greeted me with your young, new-sprung life. You ran across the meadows in my light, my delight. You grew, through my life-giving power, like a lily of the field. You gathered bluebells and made daisy chains. My never-failing power warmed your young limbs and my unseen energy sustained and formed you. It was I who caused the bluebells to bloom for you and the cherry tree to blossom. I who ripened the wheat to nourish you and the strawberries to delight you.

'The Son of Man must be raised up, as Moses raised the serpent in the desert, so that all who look upon him shall be healed.' And so too, I who energise your life on earth must be raised up, new every morning, the pivot at the centre of the circle of life. In me you live and move and have your earthly being. Yet look beyond me, for I am just a sign and a symbol of the source of all energy. I prepare your way, by nurturing your earthly life, but One comes after me who was before me, who is infinitely greater than I, and in him is the source of everlasting life.

And as I am raised, by his power, each morning above your horizon, so he too will be raised up on a tree, on a distant hill, at the edges of your vision. Look upon him, though you will want to avert your eyes, so terrible is the sight. Dare to look upon him, as the Israelites looked upon the serpent in the desert. Look upon him and live.

For a short time he is with you, and then the clouds receive him out of your sight. So too the clouds obscure my light from you and your days are often grey and overcast by care and sadness and despair. Know, on days like that, that I have not moved even a fraction out of my accustomed course. What you have seen and rejoiced in on the bright shining days is no less there for you on the days of dark and shadow. My life-giving energy is not deflected by a blanket of cloud. I continue to sustain you, whether you see me, and feel me, or not. Your sight and your feelings make no difference to my power and my reality, and my power means well with you.

He too, the Son of Man, will be taken from your sight, but his spirit will flow through you. You will neither see it nor hear it, but you will know its warmth and its joy and its power, in which you will live and move and have your eternal being.

Don't be angry with the clouds that come between us. They are being what they were created to be and carrying out the task for which they were appointed. They bring the rain that waters your earth and makes it fruitful. They too must be raised, out of the teeming seas, so that you might live. And they too, in their turn, must fall to the earth and be lost in the dark soil, to set free the hidden secrets of the seeds.

They fall, and I fall too. Back into nowhere, back beyond the horizon of your day, beyond the limits of your life, beyond your understanding, turning your light into darkness and your life into death. He too, who always is, shall be buried like me, beneath the dark earth, beyond the limits of your senses. And there he shall lie, until the dawn, until every hidden seed is ready for daybreak.

Rest in the darkness. Trust in the unseen power of the sinking sun and the falling rain and the buried seed. And listen, as you dream, to the music of the mill-race . . .

The Song of the Mill-Race

Lift up your eyes to the hills. There is my beginning, and in my beginning is your beginning too. My song is yours. From high above, from far beyond, from deep below, we have our hidden sources.

My mountain source was not, in time past, nor is to be, in time to come, but is, unchanging and unchanged. As long as I flow, my source *is*. As long as my source is, I flow.

I know not myself the hidden place from whence my source springs. Yet day by day, through time, I flow. First tiny trickles and damp mossy places. Then stronger, fuller, deeper, with every day I flow, with every mile.

Something in me longs eternally to be one with the Greater Thing in which I truly am. That longing impulse propels me constantly towards an ocean homing, there to lose myself to become perfectly what I truly am. The water seeks the ocean and the ocean is the water.

Then the rising, and the clouding and the raining. An end-less cycle. Life-cycle upon life-cycle. With purpose, or without? Its purpose lies beyond my understanding. I only know the impulse of my being, to rise in the spring, to flow in the stream, to spill myself into the ocean.

I die an ocean death and am buried in the immensity of waters. I rise again and am received into the cloud, and the cloud releases the droplets of my life-giving spirit upon the waiting earth with its secret seeds.

I obey my inner law, and I mirror my maker in his birthing and his living, his dying and his rising, his giving and enlivening and empowering.

But here, by the mill, the needs of humankind have made a complication in my flow. I am divided here. Part of me flows on, by the shortest route, to the waters of the estuary. Part of me

is diverted into the mill-race, to take a longer and more dangerous course.

There is tension in the parting. My eternal nature strains for home. But others' needs divert me to a fearful falling. I catch my breath and entrust my living spirit to the gaping drop and the thrashing clutches of the turning wheel. I am destroyed, dashed into a thousand fragments, churned and frothed and frightened. The needs of humankind exact a heavy price from my once undivided spirit.

The detour becomes my reality and I almost forget that my deeper stream flows on, uninterruptable. I almost forget that there *is* a deeper flow. My present reality and the thrashing, churning wheel seems all there is. My whole consciousness becomes engaged in the matter of the mill. Some days I meet the challenge with a defiant thrill and all the urgency of the adventure. Some days I yearn for an ending and for peace.

And then, as suddenly as it began, the parting ends and that which was to be accomplished has been accomplished. The wheel has turned another cycle, the stones have ground another round of grain, the world has eaten another day's bread and I rejoin my destined course and flow freely once again towards my destination.

And in my homing is my next departing, back to the cloud, to fall softly upon the high places of my hidden source. To fall and rise again. To flow and to divide again. Resting for a while along my way, in the stillness of the millpond, where the evening shadows fall and the branches of a tree dip gently in my darkening depths and the crab-apple sings its lullaby . . .

The Song of the Crab-Apple Tree

Son of the sun and daughter of the water I came to birth beside the mill, on the hillside, by the mill-race. Out of the warmth and the wet my secret seed sprang to life and was made visible above the earth. In the light and the moisture I grew in stature. My roots reached deep, seeking the ground water that held me in being. My branches stretched themselves in a new awakening, to embrace the skies that beckoned me to beyond myself.

Springtime decked me in my bridal dress, to receive the fruitmaker. Through the summer I brooded in the heat, nursing the new thing into life. When the autumn mists cleared and the sun lay low upon me, an exhausted lover, my swelling fruits ripened, burst and dropped to the earth. Each year I offered this, my sacrament of life, each year more fully and more deeply.

> Then came the storm.
> The storm smashed my Eden-world to pieces.
> The storm destroyed my dream.

My yearly ritual offering of life was made real and permanent and final. I fell, and could not rise again. I broke, and there was no healing. My story was ending where it had begun, deep in the dark soil. I had reached for the skies but found only the earth. I lay helpless, in the fearful memory of the storm.

The miller cried for my fall. He shook his fist at the departing storm and he stood where I had stood. And where his tears fell a new thought came into being.

'The tree has always been a part of the mill,' he thought, 'as long as anyone can remember. Let the tree remain part of the mill, therefore. It has fallen and it lies useless and helpless. I could chop it up and burn it on my fire. I could burn it, yet, though it has fallen hard, I remember its long years of being true to its nature, growing and yielding, shading and delighting. Let it not, therefore, be burned, but let it become a new thing.'

I felt the miller's hands pass over my aching, dying limbs. I had to submit to his will. I surrendered my will to his.

The miller's tools were terrible, yet I had no choice. And there was promise in the terror. There was a breaking and re-forming that was needful for the transformation. Yet, had I been free to choose my path, I would have fled the miller's workshop and the anguish of my re-making.

He held me, like a newborn baby in his hands, and showed me to his friends.

'This is just the right wood for the teeth of the drive wheel,' he told them. 'See how hard and durable it is, how I have worked it so that it fits like a wedge in the wheel. As the water falls upon it, it swells and wedges itself ever more firmly, and its hardness takes the strain of the wheel, turn after turn, day after day, year after year. The sun has hardened it well through the years, to withstand the battering of the wheel, and the water will mould it firmly into its new place in the circle of life.'

I lay, exposed and vulnerable in his hands, where all might see my shame and all might look upon the new thing that the miller had in mind.

I let him fit me carefully and gently in my place along the

rim of the sturdy drive wheel that was driven by the axle of the mighty waterwheel outside the mill, and in its turn, propelled the shaft that drove the millstones high above me. He lingered as he left me there.

'Friend Crab-apple,' he murmured, 'you will miss the clouds and the grass and the sparkling stream, as you labour here in the dark heart of the mill. Your wood that once raised its arms in joy to heaven will be bruised and battered by the constant impact of the waterwheel that drives you. You will wonder what purpose you are serving buried here in the heart of things, seeing nothing, understanding nothing. I must ask you, fallen friend, to trust me for the meanings and the promise of the harvest.'

I saw the tenderness in his eyes as he fixed me in my place.

> 'With sweat on your brow
> Shall you eat your bread
> Until you return to the soil
> As you were taken from it.
> For dust you are
> and to dust you shall return.'

The words were hard, but his gaze was tender.

Then, heavily, painfully, the great waterwheel ground into motion. The torrent thundered and the wheel's blades engaged with mine. The weight was like the weight of the world. There was no escaping the engagement. This would be my place of being, until I should be no more, and the waterwheel would cease its turning. The weight flattened my hopes into despair.

Years passed and the storm became a memory. I can hardly remember a time before my fall. Just a distant glimmer through the gaps in the mill walls, of a time when things were different. Perhaps I was never anything but a tooth in a toothwheel.

And yet, my father sun and mother water still know me, still soak me and dry me day by day, as if to say: 'We give you all we can. For the rest you must trust the miller.'

And the wheel turns and the water thunders and the millstones grind.

The millstones grind, soft balance to the thundering water. The millstones hum the melody of distant hills. I feel the forever-pain of the engagement and the sick rotation of the blades, but always, somewhere there, above me in the upper storeys of the mill, I hear the millstones' melody . . .

The Song of the Millstone

Before time was I was fire and energy, light and speed. Through space I came hurtling, a ball of fire. Speeding, cooling, slowing, settling, hardening. The very energy of my creator was in me, propelling me into separateness of being, to my place in the cooled earth. I have that of my creator in me. I am the rock, the stronghold and the fortress. Bound and firm and forever.

Walk on me, lean on me and I shall hold you sure and certain. Build on me and you shall not fall. I am your fixed point and the point beyond which you cannot go.

Fall on me, and I will split you open, like a broken husk, but only to release your secret seeds.

Break yourself upon me and I will crush you into fragments, but only to set free your hidden self.

Earth cooled. Life formed. Men and women walked and toiled and rested, seeking, sighing and rejoicing. Using eyes and mind, sharp, observant. Using hands, quick and nimble. Using earth's gifts to govern earth and make it fruitful.

They found me hidden in the rock face, hewed me, formed me, appointed me to carry out their tasks. From gritstone hills they quarried me, carried me, planed and shaped me.

And now I spin again and sing my song. As I spin, at the bidding of my neighbour wheel and my neighbour water, my spirit spins with the memory of my first spinning flight of birth.

In the water torrent I remember the running streams of home, in the gritstone hills.

When the sun's light rises, I feel the first light's rising over newborn earth. When its shadows lengthen I know again the darkening moors and the high places of my lonely home.

We spin together, two millstones, immovable object and irresistible force. Two gritstone faces, spinning with the water's energy, burning with the fire of our encounter, remembering those first and distant fires, now locked solid in our hardened hearts.

We spin at your command, our miller. We spin to do your will. We would not harm the grain. We mean no harm to what you pour between our gaping jaws. We cannot help our hardness. Our all-consuming fire has turned to all-consuming stone.

You hear our sorrow for the pain of the grain, for the crushing and destroying, and you weave your promise and your hope into our song:

> 'Your molten fires have hardened into death, and yet that death shall be the means of life, and the grain shall be flour

and the flour shall be dough and the dough shall rise and find the fire again. And the stone that was dead and buried in the gritstone hills shall become a cornerstone, for the making and shaping and baking of life. It shall bring forth the new thing, out of the jaws of death.'

Let the wheat sing its song. Let the wheat take up the story ...

The Song of the Wheat

My waking was out of a deep sleeping, deeper than memory, more distant than hope. An impulse of love shocked me into life. A shaft of warmth dissolved me into being.

There was a birth-struggle. My living energy was surrounded by the clay of the fields, wet with winter, and cold. No easy yielding, but a hard coming-to-be. Yet the outcome of the struggle was never in doubt, for I knew that life was on my side. I could feel it in every fibre of my being.

In the end the soil was glad that I had come to be, and held me firmly in its arms, like a nurse, while I grew. And the water fed my roots and the sun ripened my green into gold and the wind caressed me, and the miller looked upon what had come to be, and saw that it was good. And as I flourished in the field, I listened to the miller's silent meanings ...

Where time is not, and place has no meaning, I *am* with the miller and the miller *is* with me. Yet there is a crying in the distance, coming closer, getting louder. And the crying fills our heart and bursts it open into tears. It is the crying of the hungry children.

While the crying continues we cannot be at peace, the miller and I, until we have found the means of bringing our peace to the crying ones. As a parent cannot sleep while the child cries, so we are awake with the hungry children ...

And even as I grew in stature and in understanding, I knew that the grain that was swelling and ripening in me would be for the feeding of many; that my grain would have to die, that theirs might live again.

On a summer day the miller walked slowly through the field. The wind made waves through my standing, swaying height, and whispered its summer song. And the love of the miller swept over me like a wave, and he said:

'Do you hear the children crying, through the wind?' And I said:

'I hear the children crying. I will go. Let it be done to me, what must be done.'

I felt the stab of pain as he plucked me from the stalk, and cast me far away, into the barren empty field, where the children cried.

'Unless you fall into their ground and are buried deep in their earth, you cannot yield the food that will end their crying.'

And when the time was accomplished, I came to birth in the empty field. I was born out of emptiness into the stony ground.

I cried with the hungry children, and I was hungry too. I was bent by the winds that flattened them and bruised by their hurts and heartaches.

Sometimes I wiped a tear away and bound a breaking heart. But I was One. And they were Many.

And always, in the distance, on the hillside, I would listen to the miller's words, carried on the winds:

'Where time is not and place has no meaning, you *are* with me, and they shall be so too. Go out and call them home, to the Harvest Supper . . .'

The Harvest Supper

Autumn came and the September sunshine cast long shadows over the mill. Blackberries ripened by the mill-race.

Through the field, the miller came walking, slowly, heavy-burdened, with pain in his eyes. Over his shoulder he carried a bursting sack of finest grain. As he walked, the bulk of the sack cast a long shadow ahead of him, darkening his way. As he walked, sweat dripped from his brow, like great drops of blood.

Three times he stumbled on the rough ground under the impossible load. And each time he gathered himself together again, shifted the weight of the sack and continued his lonely journey.

It was a strange prelude to a harvest supper.

The mill was silent and expectant. The waterwheel stood still. The mill-race held its breath. The crab-apple teeth of the drive wheel rested from their continual engagement with the water and the wheel. The millstones lay, hard and heavy, each upon the other.

Evening fell upon the mill-garden, and the darkness gathered, and the gloom. It was a brooding silence, incubating that which cannot be spoken.

The miller stopped beside the mill-race. In a moment that lasted eternally, he opened the sluicegate and set the mill-race in motion. The torrent was released. Slowly the waterwheel began to turn, like an instrument of torture. One by one the crab-apple teeth of the drive wheel were brought into engagement. Gradually the millstone started to revolve.

And the sun shaded its face against what it must witness.

Slowness turned to speed, and the speed was sick and dizzy and deadly. The crying of the hungry children turned into a baying, like that of wolves. And the speed and the clamour spiralled like a tornado, drawing all the garden into its deadly draught, drawing life into death.

And in a final massive effort of love, the miller took the sack of finest grain, the first-begotten and beloved grain, and thrust it between the gaping jaws of the millstones. And the grain was crushed, and ground to powder, and destroyed.

The sun sank behind the horizon, declaring: 'It is accomplished!'

And the crying stopped, and there was silence in the mill-garden.

The miller's daughter gathered up the pure new flour, and she kindled fire in the emptiness and the coals burned red, fierce, making the new thing, baking the new bread, from the surrendered grain.

One by one they came to the harvest supper. And then in tens, and hundreds. In thousands they came, hands outstretched, hearts exhausted, to the miller's table.

The miller rose to his feet, and in his eyes there was a deep darkness and a bright joy. He bade the children come to the table. He raised his eyes to the skies and said the blessing, holding the first-baked loaf in his hands – raw energy of creation changed into bread.

'I give you of my very self,' he told the hungry children. 'It is given that you might live, and live abundantly.'

And he broke the bread, and gave it to them.

There was bread for all, and when all had eaten, the miller gathered twelve baskets of scraps from the mill-green.

When the harvest supper was over, and all were filled, the miller's daughter walked disconsolately through the silent mill.

'What are you looking for?' her father asked her.

'The finest grain has been lost,' she cried. 'Ground to powder, crushed into dust, and lost.'

'The finest grain is no longer here, as it used to be,' her father answered. 'But the life that is in the grain can never be destroyed. It will be given a new and unimaginable fullness. Go to your room in the upper storey, and wait at the window. Wait and watch. Listen for the song of the steam . . .'

The Song of the Steam

It was cold and oppressive in the upper-storey room, where the miller's daughter sat, grieving for the grain and the anguish of the crushing, and fearful for the future. There was time to think. She thought of her life and the years that had passed. The thoughts passed through her mind like the mill-race, and like the mill-race, the stream of her thoughts divided into a complication.

With one part of her mind, she thought of the fires that burned in her heart, sometimes soft and tender as a candleglow, sometimes fierce, destructive as the sweep of a forest fire. Flames for warming; flames for consuming. She thought of the love that glowed in her heart, like embers that might leap to life. She thought of the lost grain, and the flame leapt. She thought of the hungry children and the flame licked the roots of her heart. Fires of passion and compassion.

With the other part of her mind she thought of the coolness of the waters of her soul. Pools of prayer and tides of caring. Empty spaces of the heart that might be filled with life-restoring rain.

Living fountains to quench the hot and thirsty fires? Living fires to scorch the secret sources of the water? Her thoughts divided, like the mill-race, into paradox and troubled complication. Like the mill-race, her heart-stream was divided.

Idly she watched, as the steam train came trundling down the track, bringing grain to the mill. She watched as the fireman stretched himself, wiped the sweat off his blackened forehead, and bent to heave another shovel-load of coal into the furnace. She watched as the engine driver leapt down from the engine and attached a long suction hose to the water supply beside the stream.

Her idle glance turned to rapt attention. She felt with the engine, felt its thirst, its need. Felt its deep satisfaction as the water coursed into the boiler. She felt with the engine, felt the fire burning in its depths. Felt its searing heat and its potential for destruction.

She knew the water and she knew the fire. They had met together in her own heart, too: longing and desiring. Her fire longed for water, lest it burn itself out in destruction. And when the water came, the fire knew it had a purpose. The fire at the heart of her needed her heart's water, not to extinguish, but for the creating of a new energy, different from both of them, yet the joint product of their separate natures.

She offered them to her stillness and her waiting: her flames' leaping and her soul's outpouring. Her longing and desiring, not just for quenching but for full-filling. For the making of the new energy, undreamed-of.

Her thought of the fires and her thought of the water were no longer divided, like the mill-race, but had flowed together to make the new power that might set in motion the coming of the new thing, as the mill-race set the waterwheel in motion.

She felt the thrill as the blast of steam rose in front of her and the train began to move.

And the steam rose and spread and became a thick white cloud, enveloping the mill and the stream and the hillside, gathering all into a new, invisible reality, settling into every crack and crevice with its tongues of water and its streams of fire.

The miller's daughter gasped, and surrendered herself to the coming of the cloud.

The Grain-Rain

When the cloud lifted, and the veil was withdrawn, there was a pregnant dewfall on the grass, on the hillside where the mill stood. The grass was thick with wheat-grains, each one a seed corn of the finest grain.

The miller's voice called out across the hillside:

'See the grain-rain. See these seed corns of the finest grain. My hungry children, let each of you receive a seed corn of the finest grain. Let me plant it in your heart. Let it yield a hundred-fold. Let it feed the world. Let it feed the starving hearts.'

After the cloud dispersed, and the veil was torn aside, a strange new clarity and brilliance transfigured the mill, turning sight into vision.

And the mill-race understood the need for its dividing.

And the crab-apple understood the meaning of its fall.

And the millstone recognised the rock and the ground of its being.

And the steam understood the nature of its power.

And the drive wheel turned to the wheat: 'Forgive me, Brother Wheat. Through my fall I have become the means of your destruction.'

And the wheat spoke softly to the drive wheel: 'You are forgiven, Friend Crab-apple. Out of your fall I have become the means of giving life back to the hungry children.'

And the sun dared to look upon the new life, rising, without averting his eyes.

And the miller's daughter ran to tell the world about the new thing that had come to be.

And the miller looked with love upon what had come to be, and saw that it was good.

♾

In the fireplace the coal shifted and sank, with a crackling sound, into the last dying moments of the fire. The bright firelight had faded into little more than a glow. The night was deep and dark, gestating a new dawn.

I made my way softly to the door of the cottage, quietly, so as not to wake the sleepers. I went out into the lane, into the silence of the night.

The day that had been so cold and windy and unpromising had yielded a clear night. Above me a sprinkling of scattered stars shone, distantly. I stood for a moment, letting the bright cold flow round the dying embers of the dream. The sky was so much larger than the earth, full of unseen realities that daylight had concealed.

The stars nodded their blessing over me. Pinpoints of light, each a world of its own, spinning through time and space, like the separate songs the mill had sung for me. Yet, not just scattered lights, but becoming, even as I stood and gazed, a constellation with a story and a meaning, that, once discerned, might be recognised and remembered. Something that I might trust, to point a way in the darkness.

THE
NECESSARY RICE

FATHER BEDE WAS TIRED TONIGHT. There was something slightly hurried about the pace of the evening service. Just a touch faster and less measured than usual. The difference was feelable rather than measurable. He apologised for the lack of a proper sermon. He just hadn't had the time to work things out today, he said. There was a hint of harassment behind his rueful smile, the weariness of an elderly and overworked man trying to look after his own parish and that of his sick colleague too.

It was the annual appeal for the protection of unborn children. His words were brief, but impassioned.

'We live in a society where an unborn child enjoys less protection than a jackdaw or a bat,' he said. I knew that he was right, but my thoughts strayed to the schoolgirl I read about in the paper, who gave birth alone, and in secret, and I felt with her the desperate panic that drove her to leave her baby in the January fields.

He appealed to us to have the courage to oppose the destruction of unborn life. I couldn't disagree, but my mind was haunted by the picture of thousands of women held captive in rape camps through life-shattering pregnancies. I wondered, too, how it feels to be raising a severely handicapped child in a society that doesn't care, and doesn't help.

He urged us to remember the traditional values of our parents and grandparents. I tried to remember, but it didn't silence the cries in the night, either from the slaughtered unborn or from their inwardly crucified mothers, who have to go on living.

The thought of traditional values took him back to the sabbaths of his own youth, he told us, when his mother had felt free to darn socks, but not to knit, and then only after due and lengthy attendance at church. I reflected about how easy it is now to slip out to the shop on Sunday to supply the needs of leisure and pleasure and be served by the overstressed mothers of small children. Much easier than terminating a pregnancy. I thought of the relative needs involved, and wondered which was the greater sin.

The service was almost over. Father Bede seemed pre-occupied. He was about to give the final blessing when he stopped short, suddenly recalling his childhood again. His face softened and relaxed. He was smiling, laughing almost, as he shared with us an incident that had obviously penetrated deeply into his imagination. His grandmother, he recalled, had called him along one Sunday morning.

'We're out of rice,' she said. 'Just slip round to Charlie's for some rice.'

He had done as she asked. Charlie, who had already been to the early morning service, had sold him the rice. Grandma received it, stiffly, with the question:

'What did he charge you for it?'

The reply brought a stinging retort from her:

'He's put a penny on it. He might well go running to church as soon as he can get there!'

'But Grandma, you shouldn't have sent me for it on a Sunday, should you?' the infant Father Bede had remarked, with more candour than discretion.

He came back, with a jolt, to the unfinished liturgy. He bowed his head over the altar before raising his hand in blessing. But before he could quite complete the action, another rogue thought seemed to cross his mind. He raised his head again, and added, almost pleadingly:

'But we *needed* the rice ... And Charlie could supply it.'

The moment of truth lit up his whole face in a mysterious mingling of protest and submission. What had prompted that heartfelt addendum, I wondered? Was he defending his grandmother, himself, or the whole fallen human race? Two short sentences, and those spoken almost in spite of himself, yet, just for an instant, his expression and his gestures had proclaimed a whole gospel.

He bent his head again, pronounced the blessing and went into the sacristy. But his words stayed behind, kindling a fire on the altar between the now extinguished candles, and dancing provocatively in sacred spaces. I stayed behind too, in the disturbing, exciting company of those words that had come straight, unbidden, from his heart. Words that, perhaps, he would not have allowed to come to birth, had he been able to abort them. Troublesome, challenging, defiant and true. They were loose now, free to live a life of their own. Their parent had thrust them into the world and here they were, speaking their own language and stating their own case:

'*We needed the rice.*'

I thought of the world's rice and its Charlies. Of so much that we need, and the desperation that can lead us to take it from wherever it can be supplied.

Scene by scene, the dancing words acted out their own impromptu drama . . .

A misbehaving child, failing to rouse any response from his parents, threw a tantrum, in a last-ditch attempt to attract their attention. Not the recommended procedure, but he needed the rice . . .

A homeless teenager crawled out of his cardboard box and walked across my mental stage. I saw him mug the old lady and convert her pension into heroin. The facts were stark and inexcusable, but the rice-hunger was too much to bear . . .

A middle-aged man and woman appeared. Steady, respectable, but both in unhappy marriages. Year after year of quiet desperation, carefully concealed beneath their gentle exteriors, erupted into the agonising abscess of a sudden, uncontrolled affair, melting all morality in its heat and breaking the heart of all it touched. They had seized the rice, at whatever inflationary price . . .

And finally a wretched schoolgirl on her via dolorosa. Alone and pregnant. Guilt-laden. Terrified. Helpless. A child burning in adult flames. She hesitated at Charlie's door . . .

Stunned shock waves pronounce sentence: no pardon for those caught in the ring of fire. No way forward for those who need what Charlie has and take what Charlie sells. And, yes, Charlie will put a penny on the rice because he knows the depth of the need. And the price will always be more than we can pay. And we will pay it, because our need is so great. And the payment will make the need all the greater.

There will never be enough rice. And every week it will cost a penny more. And Charlie will go to the early service and be saved. And we will not dare to go to church, but wander instead ever deeper into the mire. And the ring of fire will come closer, and closer. And the best-intentioned statements of accepted morality will start with exhortation and end with words of pleading . . .

'*Lord, we needed the rice.*'

A kind of calm descends on the dancing words, settling their frenzy. In the stillness there is space for one more Word.

Someone walks through the sabbath fields, plucking stalks of corn. He can hear the cries of the hungry ones. He promises to satisfy the rice-hunger at its source. Eventually he comes to the place where the shattered schoolgirl still hesitates, sobbing, at Charlie's door. There is infinite compassion in the voice that warns against Charlie's quick fix and the hand that wipes away her tears and holds out the possibility of real solutions, still concealed in bread and wine, and in the depths of those he calls his friends. One Word, that brings meaning to all other words and

breaks through the ring of fire, beckoning us to a new rice-harvest, daring us to make Charlie redundant.

By now, Father Bede will be home again. Or perhaps he may be out on yet another mercy call, ministering to another of Charlie's customers. He may be feeling frustrated and in-adequate. Possibly reproaching himself for not having prepared a sermon for tonight's service and worrying about what he will say to tomorrow's congregation. Quite probably he will never know that when, in his weariness, his words fragmented into pleading, another Word broke through, from a man in the fields, with love in his eyes, and an ear of corn between his fingers.

CONVERSATIONS
WITH
A PUMPKIN

I MET MY INNER PUMPKIN during the course of a winter walk with a friend, one chilly January afternoon. I was laughingly comparing my physical features, following an over-indulgent Christmas season, with my spiritual constitution, which often feels like a thick wall of baggage and accessories round the outside, and a large empty space on the inside.

Just as light-heartedly, my friend remarked: 'You sound like a spiritual pumpkin!'

The odd thing about this wholly forgettable exchange of laughter was that I didn't forget it. The thought of pumpkins kept on and on coming back to me during the days and weeks that followed. Sometimes it made me smile. Sometimes it made me think. Eventually, it made me pray! 'Am I really a pumpkin?'

I demanded of God. 'And if so, is that what I want to be? Is that what *you* want me to be?'

It was after weeks of this pumpkin-pondering that I began to glimpse something of what the pumpkin – and perhaps God, and my friend – were trying to tell me that January afternoon on a Welsh hillside. Something to do with growing and changing. Something to do with the things of earth becoming the stuff of heaven.

The pumpkin patch

Once I gave him half a chance, my new-found pumpkin-friend took the first opportunity to lead me back to my beginnings. We sat down there together for a while in the pumpkin patch, along with the leeks and cabbages and beans. It was a garden allotment, and the word 'allotment' seized my attention. I too had come into the world with a particular, unique 'allotment' of physical and social space in which to do my growing, and with an allotment of physical features and other, less visible characteristics, the legacy of my parents' genes. For better or for worse, this was the soil which, with the passage of time and the blessings and afflictions of various weathers, would turn into my personal pumpkin. My circumstances would, quite literally, be turned into 'me' – or at least into the outer layers of this person I call 'me'. And I found it strangely consoling to reflect that pumpkins often grow best on rubbish heaps.

Gradually my tiny pumpkin began to grow. It became a bigger and bigger pumpkin, taking more and more of what it found around, to create a bigger and bigger presence of itself in the external world. This presence took on the shape of a large orange ball. It was like a mirror of my ego-self taking shape. It fed on the external, and had just two instincts: to *expand* and to *defend*. My ego-self is just like that, I realised. It thinks that if it fails to grow it is 'nobody', and if it fails to defend itself it will be destroyed.

And so, for me and my pumpkin, the mysterious journey of

life seems to begin with this expanding, hard-shelled, soft-centred orange ball. It is driven by the need, first to survive, and then to expand and lay claim to my bit of the planet, if not a bit more if possible.

It's beautiful, but what do you do with it?

Thankfully, most of us don't spend all our lives in this stage. It's a rare human pumpkin that doesn't, sooner or later, ask itself: 'What am I about?' My pumpkin-friend sat patiently alongside me in the patch while I grappled with these questions.

'My relationship with this orange ball I'm growing into is very mixed,' I confided in him. 'A love–hate relationship at the best of times. For one thing my orange shell is never quite as attractive or well-shaped as everyone else's. The gardener usually passes me by in his rounds, and it's always my neighbour further down the patch that he stops to admire. Come the time for the harvest festival and the vicar never puts *me* on the altar – I'm just about good enough to be packed in boxes for the needy of the parish.'

There was a silence between us. A thoughtful silence . . .

'So why is it,' I continued, 'that, trapped in this inadequate round ball of myself, that lets me down in every comparison, I still find it necessary to defend it to the hilt? I dress it up and care for it like a favourite doll. I feed it with the best morsels I can get, and if it still doesn't come up to scratch, I make dressing-up outfits for it. I learn to disguise it – to make it look bigger and better, or at any rate different. Or, more often, I have to prune it and starve it to make it into a more acceptable shape – one that fits the general idea of "perfect" in a pumpkin world. And when I've spent most of my waking energy doing all of these things, I'm still left with the night-time thoughts: Is there anything inside? And if there is, what is it for?'

There was a low-pitched murmur from somewhere to my left, where my inner pumpkin sat. 'Soup,' he commented succinctly. 'And space.'

'Is that all there is by way of a destination for my beautiful orange ego-self?' I asked, petulantly. 'Is it just about pumpkin soup, to keep me going through the long hard winter of life? And when that's eaten, just the empty space inside?'

'Choices!' the inner pumpkin rumbled again, at my side. And the comment hung there in the air between us for a few minutes, pregnant with possibility.

'Well,' I mused, 'if all I'm about is making soup, I guess there is a question about whether the soup is just for me, or whether there is any to spare for others. I may not be over-impressed with my pumpkin-shape, but there will always be pumpkins in the patch who are smaller and less well nourished than me. Whatever I have stored up, through the years, inside my orange shell, some of it may actually be destined for the use of others.' I paused for a while to think over how I felt about this. All the effort to grow into a bigger and better pumpkin was going to backfire on me. I could see it coming. I could feel the challenge hovering overhead. 'The bigger the pumpkin, the more soup for others!'

'And when the soup is cooked, eaten and forgotten, and only my empty space is left behind, I have another choice,' I continued, quite excited by all this potential hidden inside my rather unsatisfactory orange ball. 'I can curl up inside it and hide. Or I can let it become a space where a candle can be lit. If I curl up and hide, the journey is nearly over. All that lies ahead is the time of rotting away again, back into the soil that gave me life. If I agree to the candle option, I will become a means of bringing light – and *delight* – to others through *their* lengthening evenings.' Which do I prefer, I found myself wondering.

I sat back on my heels at this point, and noticed just the flicker of a smile cross the round face of my inner pumpkin, who had sunk down in a satisfied posture among the compost to enjoy my search for meaning.

'So I *do* have choices,' I told him, while he continued to pretend nonchalantly that the whole debate had nothing to do with him. 'I have choices about what to do with my fullness: to keep or to share. And I have choices about what to do with my emptiness: to drown in it, or to let it be a space for giving light to others. Neither choice offers personal immortality! I have reached the point of realising that however beautiful my orange shell may be, it is not for ever.'

'Seeds,' my pumpkin-friend grunted from the depths of the compost. 'Lots and lots of seeds . . .'

Of course, I thought to myself. How stupid of me. Pumpkins are full of seeds. Dreams of immortality took off again, fuelled by the very idea. Only to be shot down by common sense. All you get from seeds is more little pumpkins, and the whole show goes round again. More soup, more space, more seeds, and always – choices!

What do you want me to do for you?

It took a few days of swimming around in my inner pumpkin soup before a memory from childhood surfaced. *Orange pumpkins can turn into golden coaches*, I recalled. All it needs is the touch of the fairy godmother. And all *she* needs is our genuine desire.

'What do you want me to do for you?' she asks gently, as she appears in the cold kitchen of the palace, when the ugly sisters have departed for the ball.

'What do you want me to do for you?' The carpenter's son from Nazareth re-echoes the words. 'What do you want, child, if not just soup and space and seeds?' The question came from somewhere inside me, and it challenged my heart.

'Not just soup, Lord,' I found myself replying. 'Not just the means to keep my ego going, and growing.'

'Not just space, Lord, but space for you and space for your world. Not just emptiness, but emptiness for full-filling.'

'Not just seeds, Lord, for more and more of the same, but the seeds of transformation.'

I had hardly uttered the word 'transformation', hardly become aware of this, my deepest desire, when the touch of something invisible upon my heart became palpable. The beautiful, well-defended orange shell of my ego-self started to melt before my eyes. Perhaps the candle was too bright. Panic flooded me, but I couldn't reverse the process that I had set in motion with that one whisper of deep desire. The process had begun, and I knew that it would take me beyond anything my orange shell could contain.

'The Cinderella inside me wants to go to the Ball,' I found myself calling out, with a passion that took me by surprise. All that felt most inadequate, most broken, most despised and rejected in me was waking up to the deep desire for transformation.

It could all be just another, grander ego-trip, I pondered. A place in heaven? An eternal perpetuation of 'me'? Such an outcome seemed to me nothing more than a highly polished pumpkin, still light years away from the vision of the Ball.

'I hope you've heard the things I didn't say, Lord?' I launched a prayer into the blue sky high above the compost heap. 'I hope I haven't left you with the wrong impression. I'm not sure I really know what I'm asking you for ...' But the desire had been acknowledged and expressed, and that was enough. A Cinderella inside me had asked to go to the Ball.

And something even deeper inside me had heard the Cinderellas of the world around me – the sick, the lonely, the destitute, the handicapped, the homeless, the single parents and the refugees, all who are the targets of prejudice, the imprisoned, the addicted, the rejected and exploited and all who despair. Suddenly there was a huge clamour: 'We want to go to the Ball,' they cried.

I turned to my silent, patient companion on the compost heap, with a realisation of shock and sudden enlightenment: 'This coach that my pumpkin has the potential to become isn't just for my own private transportation,' I told him. 'God seems to have hired it in advance as part of his fleet to carry his guests, the neglected ones, to the Ball. He's got our pumpkin coaches all lined up as coaches of transformation long before we ourselves have realised that they can be anything other than pumpkins. They are spoken for before they are there!'

The hidden agenda

The truth is, I began to realise, that my pumpkin has a hidden agenda. All through the years when I thought life was about serving me and my ego-self, making myself as big and as attractive as possible, defending myself against anything that might not mean well with me, my real self was being prepared for quite a different mode of being.

In my conscious ego-self, my highest aspiration was to be chosen to represent the pumpkin patch when harvest festival came round. In the deeper, unconscious layers of my being, where my real self dwells, a hidden Cinderella was crying out for something much more precious. She was longing to find the source of perfect love, and to be joined to that source of love for all eternity, to become a part of it, to become a flow of love herself. What's more, my own deep-down Cinderella was not on her own! It was becoming obvious that my own Cinderella and the Cinderellas of all the world are *one*. My Cinderella can never go to the Ball unless we *all* go!

'This harmless-looking vegetable that I call *myself*,' I mused, 'whose sole apparent purpose is to keep me well fed, well defended and well thought of, turns out to have a quite different agenda, that I would never have guessed at in my wildest dreams. All along it knows that it is really a golden coach, with a very definite mission, to carry me and all creation from here to eternity.'

My pumpkin-friend twitched his eyebrows at the mention of 'harmless-looking vegetable', but he resisted any temptation to interrupt me in my musings.

'And the irony is that the pumpkin does *need* its shell,' I went on. 'My ego-self is not just something that never should have been and must be got rid of as quickly and firmly as possible. No, it is the necessary carrier of my real self. It is the holder of what transcends itself, just as the natural creation carries the transcendent reality of God who made it and holds it in being. You could even say that our ego-self is a sacrament of our real self – both pointing towards, and bringing about the greater eternal reality of who-we-are. The pumpkin is a sacrament of the golden coach, which will take us beyond ourselves, to transformation.

There was the slightest hint of a satisfied sigh from the little ball of wisdom sitting beside me on the compost heap. It only served to fuel my rising enthusiasm for the vision of what a little seed can become. Who would ever guess that a mere seed holds the secret of this hidden agenda?

Seeds too have a choice. They can grow into more of the same. Or they can be seeds of transformation. The sort of seeds that have to fall into the ground and die, before they can bring forth the New Thing.

If I could hold the very first acorn in my hand, I reflected, nothing could lead me to guess that it has an oak tree inside it. Just as surely, if I could hold the seed of my true self in my hand, nothing but faith would lead me to guess that it has a fragment of God inside it. A Godseed. A unique essence of life that has never been seen or held or known ever before in all creation. A little Cinderella-splinter of the Lord of all creation. Just one little splinter. But without it the Ball cannot begin, and the Kingdom cannot come. Heaven awaits our answer, as surely as it waited for Mary's 'Yes'.

Our pumpkin selves feel, most of the time, like the whole of our lives. They feel like the whole story of what we are about. The grand illusion of our ego-self is to convince us that this orange ball is all we have to live for. But inside the life of our pumpkin, an eternal day is waiting to dawn. In that new dawn, our creator is waiting to welcome that unique person we are becoming – the only one who fits the glass slipper that he holds in readiness for our arrival.

There is a sudden gurgle of laughter next to me, from my pumpkin-friend. He seems to find it funny that I needed so long to work out something that is so self-evident from where he is sitting! He winks at me, and then does a little somersault for the sheer joy of watching me crawl, exhausted, but contented, across the finishing line of my ponderings. Standing on his head, he grins at me, to prove that pumpkin shells are more than meets the eye . . .

And gently, laughingly, lovingly, God turns things upside-down too. The pumpkin existence we thought was life turns out to be just a fleeting day. And the day we dance in the Prince's arms turns out to be life in all its fullness.

PAN PIPER

I T'S A GLOOMY CLASS OF A DAY. The kind of day that makes you feel the sun will never shine again. And inside my mood isn't much better. I put on a CD to distract myself from the depressing thoughts that seem to be lurking in the corners of my mental attic. 'Praise Him on the Pan Pipes' the label reads. Do you *want* to be praised on the pan pipes? Is that really the mood we're in today? What does praise mean anyway? Someone once suggested to me that I praise you when I delight in you and your creation – all of your creation, including the dark bits and the dull days. And that I serve you when I attend to your presence in everyone I meet. The thought took root in me somewhere and never quite goes away.

But today I don't even delight in the music or pay it much attention. If I can't do it for the music, how can I do it for you, Lord? I close my eyes in prayerlessness, conscious of the deep sadness of empty space inside me. The city streets are thick with dust. Layer upon layer of the ashes of our dreams. I let myself fall into the fruitless, formless darkness, either to wallow in the pain, or to sink beneath it. Yes, I'm unconvinced by all the good advice to rise above it. I'm going to sink beneath it . . .

I drift slowly down through the familiar tangle of distraction and frustration. I want to hit each rising thought over the head until it lies senseless and stops tormenting me. Today the tangle is full of unseen enemies that terrorise my soul with their lurking and brooding.

But the music doesn't give up. It flows on like an undercurrent in these unspoken altercations with my rebel thoughts. The undercurrent swells and starts to take over. The darkness is full of pan pipes. A slim, dancing figure is there, playing his own pipes, dancing through the tangles as if there were no such thing as snakes or brambles.

Pied Piper, what are you doing in my wilderness, with your unsuitable clothing and inappropriate behaviour? Your cloak is

a patchwork quilt, like Joseph's – a coat of dreams. Many-coloured. Every-coloured. Like the world. You are dressed in the world. All the colour and diversity of the world. The whole great ragbag of the world. You skip in front of me. The only word is 'tantalising'. Your smile is an imp's grin, challenging the pulsing tensions of my soul, drawing me onwards, wherever you lead. At first your tune is like a serenade, to win over and soothe, to tempt into hopefulness. Then your whole body is the melody, and your whole melody is movement, light and free.

⚭

I am compelled to follow you – irresistibly drawn and hardly noticing where you are leading. We skip up steps and down, in and out of dark alleyways, sinister spaces, underpasses, subways, subterranean car parks, dirty corners of city streets. Such a dancing journey is made for many, and soon your One becomes our Many. Like some crazy party dance, we follow you to where we never intended to go.

Past the open windows of an office block. The smell of despair comes out of them like a dark cloud. Eileen is critically ill with cancer. Every time her colleagues go up or down the back staircase they remember how she would go there for a quick smoke. They hear her friendly voice. They remember the joke they shared last time they saw her. They remember her compassion for others, the heartache in her own life. They shiver inwardly as they think of her fear now, and her loneliness.

The redundancy announcements are due. This time it will hit them. All the rumours are pointing that way. Some are deeply anxious. They have young families and they don't know how they'll cope. Others are resigned to the thought and just want it to be over. A shadow of private exhaustion travels across Mike's face. He has been carrying the anxiety for the whole department, thirty human lives, thirty dependent families, for weeks, under the seal of silence imposed by his managerial position. He has been fighting their corner, knowing that if he fails, he will be the one who will have to make those impossible choices. He has been carrying your cross, though I guess he doesn't know it.

For a moment there is calm in the anxious busy-ness and the unspoken tensions. Some move instinctively towards the window and briefly glimpse a call to something stronger than fear, dimly hear strains of music that once brought their limbs and hearts to life. One of them unaccountably feels the need to write a note to Eileen. Another makes Mike a cup of coffee, and delivers it with a friendly smile.

The dance goes on . . . To a street party in the underground car park, where Steve has his mattress. Poor, alcoholic Steve. He cries when he remembers the beatings in the children's home. He flinches when he recalls the brawls in prison. When he is sober, he wonders what might ease the aching hunger in his belly. Then he drowns the thought and falls back against the hard brick wall. A shadow comes to rest across his face, and rouses him. This time it isn't just the clink of a coin into his shabby little box, with its meagre sprinkling of coppers. This time someone has bothered to stop and say 'Hello. Can I get you something to eat?' Another human being has noticed his humanity. He laughs when he hears the piper calling. There is delight in his eyes.

... On through the underpass, and Alan, half crippled by arthritis, jumps up to join the dance. He had thought it was the end of the line. Nobody noticed his lovely Scottish accent, until a passing shopper stopped to speak to him. No one knew that he still dreams of Aviemore, and the wife he lost, until someone bothered to stop and ask him where he came from. No one could have guessed how much he longed to dance again, as once he danced in other times and better places. Until a friendly greeting made his toes tingle to the piper's tune. Truly, you make lame men walk. You pipe them into life.

Jim is old now, and frail. His breaths come hard. Each one costs a stabbing pain. He sits smoking at the top of the stairs just outside the entrance to Woolworths. Hour on hour. Day on day. Week on week. Through long coldness, cold loneness. He thinks he is past surprises, but dead despair flickers into something like a possibility. A child stops to stroke the little dog who sits patiently at his side, day by day, and shares the scraps that fall from the hands of the well fed. 'What do you call your dog?' the child asks. And his mother fumbles for her purse. While the music lasts, the pains recede, the breaths come easy.

Further on, Patrick sits huddled in a dark alleyway next to Boots. He is sunk into permanent silence. As you pass, his huge, young, innocent white face rises like a full moon out of the night sky of his great black coat. Eyes, full of tragic hurting, follow your movements. It's lunchtime, and a young assistant from the shop slips out into the road and brings him a sandwich from the store, and a warm drink she has made for him. The unexpected warmth draws him out of apathy and into the orbit of life. As children run in and out of a skipping game with light but measured steps, the cold white of his sad round face moves into the focus of your radiance and joins the great creating dance.

You slip through the crowds at the station, and tumble joyfully between the buskers until you gather up Tim. Tim is far too young for the life he has fallen into, huddled at the kerbside, nursing his guitar. There is music in Tim too, and his music resonates with yours. He comes to life when a student smiles and tells him how much she likes his song. I catch a glimpse of your patchwork coat flying through their brief conversation. His strong young arms reach out to you, in simple pleasure that you bothered to say 'Hi!' 'I'll play you a tune,' he says. You have set his dreams to music and his eyes shine.

~∞∞~

In the market-place Jake is in his usual spot, with his begging bowl, and the little cardboard notice telling the world that he is homeless and hungry. The passers-by are not hard-hearted people. Not at all. They have smiles for him, and sympathy. They know what he needs. But they don't really have it either. They have just about enough to keep their own heads above water. Next week it might be some of them sitting here in Jake's place. They know that, and they are afraid of their own powerlessness. Jake sits and thinks. He has nothing left to lose and everything to hope for.

It seems easy and natural when you come to squat there beside him. Another homeless chap, he thinks, as he smiles a shy welcome. I sense the solidarity between the two of you. For a while you sit there in silence together, resting from the dance, just watching the scene, soaking up the atmosphere, noticing the buzz of the market.

When you eventually speak, your question surprises Jake.

'What are you begging for?' you ask him. 'What would you like me to give you?' You don't look as though you *have* anything to give. And suddenly Jake doesn't know what he really wants. He stares at you in amazement, as if you were some kind of fairy godmother in disguise, who might be about to turn his pumpkin into a royal coach.

'Maybe I *can* do some transforming,' you smile, reading his thoughts. 'What would you like me to give you?'

He could have asked you for a few coppers. That was what he normally did, if anyone stopped close by with a look of generosity on their faces. But then his thoughts deepened. He could have asked you for a resolution of any, or all, of the many problems and difficulties he was facing. He thought of them, one by one, and you watched the thoughts, without commenting. He could have asked you to touch the lives of one, or all, of a number of particular people that he cared about. He named them to you, one by one, and you received their names with quiet acceptance.

Then he glanced at that notice that lay in front of his begging bowl. 'Homeless and hungry.' He couldn't put into words the feelings it was expressing. There was just an unspeakable longing to be finally and permanently 'at home', and a yearning for something beyond himself to fill the hungry empty space inside him.

You put your arm round his shoulder, and drew him closer. 'You're right,' you told him. 'I don't have much to give. I'm homeless too. I'm on the road. But at least we can share our bread.'

It was then that Jake felt compelled to look deeply into the face of the one who spoke to him with such warmth and authority. It was weather-tanned, gaunt with the hollows of its own hunger, marked with the lines of hard living. But it was so alive with love. Your eyes were like flames that seemed to be the source of all warmth. He saw in your face that inexpressible gift that he knew he wanted more than all the money or the blankets or the food, or the solutions to the world's problems.

'Pan Piper,' he begged, 'just give me your love. I think that is all I really need.'

It was a moment of transformation, after all. The pumpkins on the market stalls didn't turn into fairy coaches, but one of the nearby stallholders caught sight of Jake and came across.

'Good to see you again, chief,' he grinned, with a familiar pat on Jake's shoulder, as he handed the two of you a small cob of bread. 'Who's your mate?' he added, glancing down at you with curiosity, as you sat there in your strange pied piper's outfit. You thanked him, courteously and warmly, and then you split the little loaf and gave Jake half. And I knew that you were breaking your very self and giving him your heart. You ate the bread together, and then you stood up and drew him to his feet.

'I have turned homelessness into pilgrimage,' you said. 'Why don't we walk on together?' Jake took your hand, gladly. He had nothing to lose. And everything to hope for. Your love, wrapped up in a little cob of bread, had drawn him back into the dance of life.

掗❃掘

The city streets are still thick with dust. It feels like the ashes of all human hope. Grey dust containing all life's hurting. The pain that begins with 'Hosanna!' and ends with 'Crucify!' Broken relationships. Broken contracts. Broken health. Broken homes. Shattered dreams and splintered people. The ash is real. Not just a symbol of repentance, but a thick, choking layer of hopelessness lying like a pall upon your once-so-lovely world. An urban desert full of ashes. We struggle through deep shifting sands of it, and the desert winds lash our faces, obliterating every trail. But somewhere through the dust storm your voice sings through: 'There are no footprints in the dust,' you say, 'but I am the Way. I am your Way here and now, minute by minute. In broken hearts and broken lives. On the backstairs, in the manager's office and on the cancer ward. I am the Way through the door by which your redundant colleague leaves the building. The Way through the door that the departing partner slams behind her as she goes. The Way through the doors to the separate tables of those who have too much and those who have nothing. Your ways are not my Way. Yet still, breaking through all the paradox, my Way leads on through your ways. Through them. With them. In them . . .'

Your song has consecrated our ashes and your dance goes on. Out of the market-place into another Monday morning. Down the High Street, gathering the margins of your world into the patchwork dreamcoat, into the captivating tune of love, that we only hear when we join our own hearts into its melody.

Your One draws up our Many and makes us one in delight, one in attending to the piper who makes us forget all lesser sensations. Delighting and attending. Attending and responding. Praise isn't so hard. We only have to dance . . .

We have heard your music, even though we had our fingers in our ears.

THE WISDOM
OF THE WOODS

❧

I'D NEVER SEEN SUCH A BEAUTIFUL CREATURE. I was working at my desk, with half an ear continually tuned in to pick up any rumblings audible outside in the road, lest I should miss the sound of the van with the expected delivery I had stayed at home to receive. It must have been one such imagined rumbling that drew me to a window at the front of the house.

But there was nothing in the cul-de-sac outside. My ears had deceived me again and I turned to go back to my desk. It was at that moment that the little flash of yellow caught my eye and I heard the tiniest tapping and flapping outside on the window-sill. My first thought was that a big bee was hovering just the other side of the glass. A bee, at this time of the year? And so big? So bright? I turned back to the window to investigate. And then I saw her. A tiny bird, small as a young wren, but with a huge yellow streak across her head like a golden pancake. A little goldcrest.

She seemed quite panic-stricken, and I felt helpless, watching her struggle to keep her balance on the windowsill. I could almost hear her wondering out loud whether her wings would carry her as far as the branches of the nearby spruce tree. The tapping ceased abruptly and ominously as she slid out of view. I looked down to the path below, ready to go down and rescue what might remain of her after her long fall. But she had mere-ly dropped onto one of the lowest branches of the tree, and I watched as she fluttered from branch to branch, until she perched at the top of the tree, like a Christmas decoration that has been stowed away all year in a box and has at last come to its moment of glory.

She looked at me and I looked at her. In her eyes were a kind of invitation. And the patch of gold on her head seemed to shine like a beacon, suggesting things unseen amid the tangle of creation, and things to be discovered. She seemed to be inviting me into her own restless searching, calling me to fly with her through the forest just beyond the reach of my own out-stretched arm – to discover the wisdom of the woods I had lived alongside for over half my life.

Then, in my imagination, this exquisitely fashioned little creature with the light of the world daubed all over her crest, came to perch on my shoulder. I didn't need to ask where we were going. She hopped ahead of me, tree by tree, through my own memories, to truths I had perhaps always known, but never seen before. She guided me on a forest trail, and, without my really knowing how, she turned my thoughts to prayers . . .

The oak

The bite of January gripped us as we made our first stop in the shadow of the vast oak tree. It has grown here, surely, for hundreds of years already, and watched human generations pass beneath its boughs like ships in the night. Goldcrest perched in its topmost boughs and bade me listen to its story coming in whispers on the wind . . .

The whispers speak of a miserable, grey day, and I feel grey and miserable, too. The wind is howling, echoing the silent howling in my soul. When I look out at the oak tree all I can see is the vast network of its branches. They form a filigree of black threads across the grey sky. At the farthest tip of each little twig, there is a slender and delicate bud, forming a minutely fine point, tightly closed, a tiny needle pointing into space. Closer to the main branch, the twigs thicken and become more sturdy, and eventually the powerful, unshakeable trunk leads down to the hidden roots.

But my gaze never really reaches the trunk. I find myself transfixed by those tiny needle-points reaching recklessly into the inhospitable sky. They seem quite dead, but in two or three months they will look completely different. They will break out into something rich and new, something green and alive and full of possibility. Another season, and they will flame with

colour, glorious in the September sunlight, helpless in the October winds, until they are once more surrendered to the winter frost.

It would be ludicrous to suggest to that fine tip at the end of the smallest twig at the crest of the huge oak, that it has any connection with deep hidden strands of life-supplying root. Relatively speaking, the hidden bud is a million miles from its root-source. If it were a sentient being, it would assert its own identity and self-sufficiency. It would be feeling now as I do, that the grey sky will never lift and the frost never thaw. If I enquired as to its wellbeing in spring, it would leap into life and tell me of its joy, and then, in September, it would cry out its autumn yearning on my shoulder, until the melancholy of November closed it up and silenced its song, apparently for ever, for its memory is short and its present mood seems all that could ever be.

If I were to tell it of the great network of root and branch of which it is the outer edge, it would not believe me. Yet here, from where I am looking, the picture is so obvious to me. To separate the bud from the root is unthinkable. I stand outside it and can see its wholeness, yet my own wholeness remains to me an impenetrable mystery. I feel like an isolated speck of matter floating undirected round a wild and frightening universe. In winter I have no memory of spring and in spring no fear of autumn. Each flow-tide sweeps me up on to a new shore, and each ebb-tide leaves me desolate on the empty beach.

I want to climb the tree and whisper to each cold, dead bud the stupendous truth, that the vast trunk of the oak, a great subterranean network of roots and a superstructure of countless branches exist to support it. Without them it would not exist. Without it, they would have no purpose. I want to reassure it that the roots will not stop feeding it, however dead it looks, that its passing moods make no difference to the life-cycle of the great oak.

Or do they? I think of the sadness engendered by the sight of a bud that fails to open in its proper season, a twig assailed by fungus or parasite, a dead branch amid a living tree. They are a kind of blasphemy that offends the whole of creation. They are a sleepless night in God's dream of the universe. Those who have understood these things speak of the way in which every discordant cell brings disorder into the entire creation, such is the interconnection that links each to all.

I think too of the deep-felt joy that wells up in me when I see the oak bursting out into its spring green, when I rest in summer beneath its spreading shade, when I marvel at the autumn blaze it kindles in my heart, and the silhouette of winter it offers me in frost and snow against the clear blue sky. The mood of every bud is my mood too. I laugh and cry with all creation, and all creation laughs and cries with me. Deep down, I understand your Truth, written out for my slow mind and senses in the great oak, that I am as surely connected to you as each lifeless bud is to that vast trunk. I, who live and move and have my being in you, can never be separated from you, never lost, never cut off from your eternal and unchanging root.

I shed my winter tears today, not that creation might be sad, but that they might fall upon creation's roots and help to nurture the leaves of spring, my own leaf and every leaf that your tree will ever bear. I offer them for your greater glory, just as each sleeping, hope-containing bud exists for the greater glory of the mighty oak, that creation might reflect and embody your eternal intention and have its being through you, with you and in you.

The lilac

Goldcrest shook herself, as if shedding the winter cold and preparing for warmer days. I found myself following her into springtime, and the mellow shelter of an abbey garden.

A warm dawn greets the eagerly awaited day of reflection. I wander quietly round the small enclosed garden sheltering in the inner courtyard of the old abbey. A few wild-looking trees fill up most of the space and spread themselves over the grass and the narrow path. The windows of the chapel glance down, as if to wonder who will ultimately claim this space, the steady, age-moulded, rain-stained stones or the thrusting exuberance of the springtime growth?

I come up against a mass of snarled-up, twisting, winding branches, occupying a whole corner of the courtyard. At first I see only the knots and tangles, as the thick arms of bark and branch jostle and push for primacy.

They remind me of a nest of snakes, such as might have insinuated their way into Eden and paralysed the tree of life. I know them for my own snakes, real and imagined, and I pull back instinctively.

They remind me of the messes of wool I used to create as a child when my mother tried to teach me to knit, patiently disentangling my every failure. I know them for my life's tangles that tighten and toughen, the harder I pull at them.

They remind me of the demoniac who called to you out of the caves, at once both desiring you and fearing you. He was the man who knew his name was 'Legion', because there were 'many of him'. I know them for the multiplications of my own compulsions and contradictions.

Yet despite the twisting snakes and wrestling branches, there is a peacefulness in the courtyard. Not a mysterious peace, particularly, but just the kind of peace that the world *can* give, when it is peopled by men and women who give each other welcoming space and loving acceptance. I am grateful for such peace. It helps me to recognise that the chaos that the snarling branches have called up into my prayer is also a place where re-creation might begin.

I reach out my hand, to touch the writhing tentacles of my inner entanglement, embodied in the branches. I feel the roughness, like the coat of a strange, untrustworthy dog, who might bite, but, today, allows himself to be approached. Not just my dog, but everybody's dog. A wider fear, a deeper need, a larger hunger than just my own.

And even as my fingers travel across the gnarled bark, I seem to become aware of a steady source of life. Somewhere beneath my feet, in unseen roots, somewhere below the surface agitations of my heart, there is a wholeness. It draws my senses beyond the immediate claims and tensions and I become overwhelmingly aware of a fragrance all around me, penetrating my pores and settling into the labyrinth inside me.

This is a lilac tree, I realise, with startling clarity and joy!

High above me, there is a trellis of green and clustering white. The blossom draws my focus beyond the snarls and tangles and the winding suffocations, to another fact: the fact of joy implicit in the fact of pain. The hidden reality of life, that has travelled up all the way from the unseen roots of me, through my mazes and my messes, to break out into a determined resurrection at the tip of every struggling branch.

And surely, I hear you murmur, what can be true for me must be true for all, can be received as a sign and a pledge of the coming of the Kingdom, steady and sure, through the aching of the ages.

The scent of lilac sheds a different kind of peacefulness upon the inner courtyards of my heart. A peace that the world *cannot* give, but which it is waiting, *longing*, to receive. Waiting like winter branches for the moment of the blossom. A peace that promises a joy that doesn't deny or cancel out the pain, but becomes its ultimate statement.

The rose and the rootstock

Spring exuberance was giving way to the haze of late summer, as Goldcrest settled triumphantly among the roses and waited for my thoughts to catch up with her flight.

We've had to cut back the climbing rose again. What a shame! Nothing is lovelier than to see that drift of delicate pink flowers clustering round the doorway, and to draw deeply on their summer fragrance.

But my gaze is drawn to the thick, sturdy rootstock, already weathered, and exposed through erosion. I seem to see a mirror of my own and the world's existence in that rootstock, and hear Goldcrest challenging me with an unexpected question: 'Where would you rather be?' she asks. 'In the fleeting blossom time of these fragile flowers, or in the dull, shapeless, weathered rootstock at your feet?'

There seems to be no contest. 'No one will look at the rootstock.' I respond. 'Everyone will admire the flowers and inhale the fragrance and touch the satin-textured petals.'

'But the rootstock,' she points out to me very gently, 'so unattractive in itself, contains all the flowers that the tree will ever

yield. It holds them safe in its gnarled arms, as surely as the egg holds the chick. The work of the rootstock is not glamorous, but necessary. Its task is to keep making beauty out of clay – to take in all that is good and life-giving from its surroundings and circumstances, and to let God's hidden mystery in its heart transform them into the eternal possibility of roses. To make the invisible visible. To make the universal into the particular, the All-Rose into *this* rose and *that* rose. In the rootstock God is continually creating the rose.'

For a few minutes a silence hangs between us. Perhaps it is this silence that points out to me that most of my life has been spent yearning for the roses, and on the whole my prayers have remained unanswered. Instead, you have taken me deep into my own roots, to the place of the All-Rose.

'Now that you have been to the rootstock,' Goldcrest continues, 'you can never again rest with a single rose, that buds today and fades tomorrow. You will grieve for the many petals in your life that will never open in your few short years, but you will always know that the All-Rose is eternally within you.'

'I really do still hope that my life may open into roses, Lord,' I tell you, 'but I have the feeling now that it wouldn't be enough any more to put them in my own vase and keep them just for my delight. If there are roses, let them be for all creation, and perhaps it won't even matter if my own eyes never see their blossom time. If I really have to choose, then let me abide in the root, with the All-Rose, and all shall be well.'

The rowan

The last of the summer warmth was fading from the hillside. The school holidays were over and a degree of autumnal peace was settling over the landscape. Beyond the hill the farmer was marking and dipping the sheep. The September sun shone fitfully, but with determination, between the darkening clouds. Goldcrest flew ahead of me and took up her position in an isolated rowan tree, heavy with berries.

Idly I stoop to pick up a fallen rowan berry, and become aware of Goldcrest's deep gaze resting on me. She senses my sadness that this perfect berry will soon rot away in the wet earth. I let the berry roll round in my hand. Suppose I knew nothing of your creation except this scarlet berry, I think to myself. Suppose I were holding the very first rowan berry in my hand, I could have no inkling of all that it might become.

Goldcrest seems to finish my thoughts for me, in her silent gaze: 'If you know the berry, you know the rowan tree which let it fall, and the rowan tree which it is destined to become.'

I look again at the tiny berry in my hand. Suppose, indeed, that I knew – *really* knew – this berry, and could see the innermost secrets of its being. Suppose I could read its hidden language and perceive all its concealed meanings. This berry has inside itself the full genetic profile of the rowan tree that it is destined to become. I can't see it, or read it, or ever encompass it with my mind. But I know it by faith. I hold its promise, as heart-knowledge.

My thoughts become prayer: '*Your* knowledge is heart-knowledge, Lord. You know, you *really* know, the fullness of the tree while it is still hidden in the fallen berry. You know the fullness of each of us, your creatures, while we are still wholly unevolved.

'I know that I am holding something sacred in my hand, here beneath the rowan tree. It will fall into this grassy bank, to be buried in the hillside, or eaten by a bird, or washed away by the river to another seeding place. It will fall and die, just as the Father let *you* fall and die, but the falling and dying will release the hidden life enclosed inside it and it will rise again into the rowan tree that it was eternally meant to be.'

I begin to tune in to just a little of Goldcrest's wisdom: 'When you see the berry for what it truly, deeply is, then you see the tree, and you see the forest that shall spring from that tree's harvest. When you see other people for who they truly, deeply are, then you see the people God is dreaming they shall become, and all that shall spring from the harvest of their lives. When you see the Son for who he truly, deeply is, then you see the Father, and you catch a glimpse of the Kingdom.'

'But the seed-knowledge is only contained in darkness,' Goldcrest reminds me, 'and only given to the eyes of faith. The darkness that nurtures the seed is pregnant with promise, and the promise starts to grow when the outer crust of fear dissolves. In the darkness of creation's mystery, that which might have come to nothing shall come to harvest.'

The spruce

I became aware, in my drowsy musings, of a sudden swaying of the boughs of the spruce tree, where this trail first began. Goldcrest had landed back on the branch from which we first set off. It was barely dawn, and the sun was just rising on a crisp, clear winter day.

It was over twenty-five years ago that we planted our Christmas tree out in the garden. The garden was barely more than a patch of raw earth then, and the home, in which we would raise a family, was still rough with building dust and the sharp edges of newness. But we celebrated Christmas properly, with a real tree, with real roots, and after Christmas we planted it, hopefully, in the front garden.

It flourished! It soon became so tall that there was no question of bringing it back into the house in later years. It had far outgrown the house!

Instead, we installed a set of coloured lights in it, which we switch on every year at the beginning of December to mark the season of Advent. These little globes of light shine through the dark nights of the darkest period of midwinter, until the Feast of the Epiphany. The lights in the tree are one way of expressing a trust in a Light that outshines every darkness, and in a coming season of growth and renewal that will always supersede winter's dying.

But today this tree has something to show me. I watch, enthralled, as the dawning of the new day gradually reveals the full height and breadth of the spruce. I catch a glimpse of the morning sun shining on one of the Advent light bulbs. It is just a momentary sparkle, and my gaze rests on the fullness of the tree itself – its swaying branches, its tender green needles, its straight and soaring crown. Then I notice the life the tree supports: the squirrels, the wrens and the wood pigeons, the beetles and the bugs. And, of course, the little goldcrest.

I think of Advent, and how all we can see then are the sparkling coloured lights that we ourselves have installed. What a delight they are, reminding us of the coming season of Christmas. It was almost possible, during Advent, to imagine that the spruce tree's whole purpose is to bear our little coloured lights. But when the year turns, and the Christmas lights are turned off, the real light of a real dawn returns. What we see then is not the bright lights in our tree, but the tree itself, in all the fullness of its life – its evergreen life.

The tree reminds me of the little lights the human race fixes in the tree of life. They take many forms: specific lifestyles and ways of doing things; philosophies that seek to make sense of life; different ways of making a spiritual journey; different religious formulations; and all the earth's many and varied traditions. They are precious in their way. Each brings its own light. Together, if we can agree to embrace our differences, they light up the darkness of our seasons of waiting and wandering. During such seasons, our little lights are all we see, and it is surely right to value and to cherish them.

But the Dawn will come. And when it does, all our lesser lights will be superseded by the Sunrise. In the Dawnlight we begin to see the wholeness of our 'tree' – our earth, the living web of being that holds each of us, and every creature, in an eternal interconnectedness. Then we will see the lesser lights for what they were: candles to light us through the darkness. And we will rejoice in the homecoming of all creation to its completeness in you.

The thorn bush

There is a tradition, recalled in the book of Judges, that the trees of the forest once gathered together to choose a king for themselves. First they asked the olive tree. But the olive tree said that in order to become their king it would have to stop producing its olive oil, so needful to all. So they asked the fig tree to be their king. But the fig tree said that in order to become their king it would have to stop producing its fruit, so sought after by all. Then they asked the grapevine to be their king. But the

grapevine reminded them that if it were to become their king, it would have to stop producing the wine that brings such joy to human life. Finally in desperation, they realised that they would have to seek a king who appeared to have no gifts to offer – a tree whose presence and produce would not be missed, and who would thus be free to serve them as their king. They came to the thorn bush. The thorn bush replied that if they were serious about making him their king, they must first take shelter among his thorns. They must know, for themselves, the meaning of the thorn bush.

Goldcrest invited me into one last flight with her, as she perched on the cold, bare earth. Her yellow crest shone like a tiny crown among the thorns. The tiniest bird of the forest had a crown to bestow, but her choice would confound my human expectations. 'So which tree would you choose to be your king?' she asked me.

I thought back over the journey we had made together.

In the bleak days of January I had learned that when I am at the point of desolation at the end of a lonely branch I am supported and held in being by the vast network of your love, and that network of love and life will bring me to new seasons and new growth. Perhaps I would choose the oak tree to speak to me in my times of desolation.

In the gentle breezes of May I had come face to face with the tortuous route that my life often travels before it discovers its destination in a crown of pure and fragrant blossom. Perhaps I would choose the lilac tree to speak to me of the joy that is born on the other side of pain.

In the warmth of the July sun I had begun to understand the secrets of the rootstock that contains all the roses that shall ever be. Perhaps I would choose the rose bush, to speak to me of my longings to be part of the deep heart of all creation.

In the mellow light of September I had discovered that to know the part with the eyes of faith is to know the whole. Perhaps I would choose the rowan tree, to speak to me in my disappointments and in my fragmentation and my falling to earth.

Under clear December skies I had seen the lights of human searching eclipsed by a Kingdom-Dawn. Perhaps I would choose the spruce tree, to speak to me in my searching for meaning and for truth.

Now it was March again, and a time for dying and for re-surrection. Goldcrest flew ahead of me, deeper and deeper into the forest. It was getting darker. She took me to a remote corner of the woods and landed on a straggling thorn bush, bare and exposed in the gloomy light. I looked at her in disbelief. Was she expecting me to take this bush seriously? Everything about it was repugnant to me. It had nothing to offer except hurting and bleeding. She had introduced me to so many trees, all potentially kings of the forest, full of wisdom and of truth. She had opened up my vision to see so much hidden harvest latent in the cold realities of life. And now, at the end of our journey, she had brought me here to a desolated thorn bush.

'You can go back,' she said. 'I won't force your choice.' I hesitated. 'But watch the sky,' she went on. 'The storm could break any minute, and where will your shelter be?'

Even as she spoke, I felt the first drops of rain fall heavily on my skin and drip noisily from the overhanging leaves. I felt suddenly deeply afraid.

You read my need in my eyes, Lord, and drew me gently closer to yourself, into the heart of the thorn bush. I barely noticed the scratching and tearing. I had no time to think back to the wisdom of the trees or the joy of the blossom or the promise of the harvest. You held me close, close enough to feel the thorns encircling your head.

We could have chosen the solid promise of the oak and the rowan. We could have settled in the consolations of the lilac and the rose. Instead, we faced the storm with only that fragile crown of thorn between us and the raging heavens. Our shelter was here in this ultimate exposure, stripped of all illusions and shaken free of the secret belief that we could do anything to save ourselves, or to fathom our own deepest meanings.

I trembled in your arms, barely daring to watch the drama that was unfolding in the forest. Every jagged branch of the thorn bush was alive with its own deadly energy, thrusting into the black sky like a charge of lightning, each one reflecting a flash of gold from the head of the companion at my side. Heaven and earth were disintegrating, and chaos was come again. Oak and spruce and rowan crashed helpless to the forest floor. Rose bushes and lilac trees blazed like so much kindling, and were laid waste. These fragile bearers of your wisdom and your truth had served their purpose and were gone. From now on, the only shelter would be that which remains when everything else is lost and left behind.

I looked up to where you hung, high on the bare tree. 'Which tree will you choose to be your ruler?' you asked me again. 'Which tree will you trust?'

NIGHT CROSSING

THE ROLLING OF THE DECK BENEATH MY FEET is all there is to remind me that I am actually at sea. Otherwise the passenger lounge makes no concession to the radical change from life on land to life on water. Its occupants – and I am one of them – are completely insulated from the alien world of wind and wave and water, of darkness and emptiness, that surrounds us on every side. We have reconstructed our land-reality here, where it can never really belong. We are making a journey, but we have wrapped ourselves in an illusion of unchangeable familiarity. Which, by the way, is a good deal more comfortable than being outside on the deck, in the night.

The live music intoxicates me, in spite of myself, and its beat connects itself insistently with the rhythm of my pulse, like an old friend who wants to dance again, but hardly likes to ask. I sit, relaxed and at ease, watching my fellow-travellers and letting my dreams roam freely in this unlikely place. In the subways of my mind, I find an untold story . . .

❦

They say that once – perhaps a long, long time ago, or maybe tomorrow – there was a remarkable crossing of the North Sea, one dark winter night. The ferry left harbour as usual. Nothing out of the ordinary was recorded in the captain's log. Like tonight, the passengers found their cabins, unpacked their overnight bags and had their meal. Then they ambled along to the lounge, noticing the heavy rolling of the deck beneath their feet, to enjoy their duty-free drinks and the live music, or even, for the bolder and more brazen, the casino.

If you had asked the ticket and passport inspectors, none of them would have remembered the man checking in. There was no record of him having driven a vehicle on board or of his being a passenger on any of the coaches. None of the stewards would have recalled checking his boarding card or showing him to his cabin. He was simply there, on board, alongside every other journey-maker, and there was no reason to be particularly surprised about that.

I could swear that in my dreamy haze I saw him sitting there in the lounge, tapping his feet to the rhythm of the entertainer's songs and laughing at her jokes, applauding vigorously at the end of every item. Something in his face and his bearing attracted attention.

He finished his pint of lager with obvious enjoyment and then smiled at me. I ought to have felt embarrassed I suppose, that he had caught me out, staring shamelessly at his so-alive face. But there was no such feeling. His smile called out its counterpart from me and our eyes met across the rolling,

carpeted deck. Not a come-along smile at all, but the smile shared between two people who have never met, yet always known each other. I knew that his smile had set off some un-expected new thing deep inside me, as the first warm days of March wake up the sleeping daffodil bulbs. I didn't understand, but I *knew*.

Nor was I the only one to experience the touch of spring-time that dark winter night, as we journeyed across a stormy, hostile sea . . .

👓

The fractious little girl had been nagging and pestering her parents all evening to take her out on deck. But her father was exhausted after driving hundreds of miles to the harbour, and her mother was busy with the fretful, whimpering baby. They were trying to relax with their gin and tonics and were visibly weary of telling their daughter that she wasn't going anywhere out of their sight, and that *they* were staying put. It was the last straw when the stranger arrived in the corner where they had settled themselves.

He sat down between them, and wished them a peaceful evening. He said it as though he really meant it. They were too surprised to think of an appropriate response. Even the baby stopped crying and the little girl's attention was held by this new and unexpected presence.

'Shall I take them out for a little walk round?' he asked, politely.

You could see a procession of outraged protests marching across their foreheads, just for a passing moment, to be followed in quick succession by smiles of amazed relief that seemed to originate from somewhere deeper than the surface levels of family tension.

'Feel free,' the father said, to his own immense surprise, and the stranger went off into the night, holding the little girl's eager hand and carrying the baby tenderly in his arms. The parents must be mad, you could have thought. Or perhaps more sane than they had ever been before . . .

⟨∘⟩

There was an incident in the disco that evening, too. Some of the teenagers had had a good deal too much to drink. The girl in the jeans and blue sweater looked nervous and very, very young. She was sitting uneasily on the edge of the bar stool, sipping her coke, when an older lad grasped her wrist and led her out into the anonymous, throbbing mass of disco-dancers. No one else noticed his companion slip a small white tablet into the girl's unfinished drink. And even if they had, no one would have thought it especially unusual. No one would have felt inclined to do anything about it.

When she returned to her place there was a stranger sitting next to her. For a moment it looked as though the older boys were going to turn nasty. But the stranger didn't wait for their permission to take the girl's drink away and order her a fresh one. If she had been able to overcome her speechless delight, she would have said that she had never tasted a coke quite like that one, or ever felt the warmth of loving concern in the way she did that night. But ugly unforgiving was etched on the older boys' faces as they withdrew into the shadows to consider how to deal with the unwelcome intervener . . .

⟨∘⟩

The temperature was rising rapidly in the casino. A tense silence gripped the onlookers, while the two men fought out their gambling war. The stakes kept rising. The property man from the better end of the city was sweeping the notes away from under the nose of the opportunist lorry driver who had already thrown his next month's wages into the jaws of his own compulsion. The atmosphere was electric. The two men eyed each other across the table, as the hostess set the wheel in motion. And again, the property man swept the notes into his bottomless pocket, and sheer despair gaped out of his opponent's eyes.

The deadlock was broken when a stranger walked calmly up to the table.

'My life for what he has in his pocket,' he said, indicating the recent victor.

'Go and play your games somewhere else,' the hostess was about to say, but found herself unaccountably inarticulate. The wheel began to spin again. The notes changed hands. All of them. Until the property man was back to square one. The stranger shifted the money quietly from winner to loser.

'Get out of this,' he said, 'and don't get into it again.'

He said it almost under his breath, and so gently, as the mother of a defiant toddler might draw her child back to his senses.

He walked slowly and calmly to the door and out into the cold night. It was dark and sinister on deck. He was almost alone out there, but not quite. Shadows, almost indistinguishable against the dark bulk of the ship, followed him silently. And from a distance we watched, aghast – the girl from the disco, the travel-weary little family, the opportunist lorry driver, and I. We watched, and couldn't do anything to stop the terrible payment of the gambling debt. And if we could have expressed our feelings, we would have said that it felt like *our* debt that was being paid, out there on the dark deck, as the boots went in and the heels crunched down on the gentle face of the stranger.

He looked at me again, one last, long, penetrating look. For a moment my fear dissolved and I moved close to where he lay. His eyes still glowed with the same warmth that had awakened the buried seeds of my heart, just hours earlier.

'Give them my love,' he commanded me.

There was no further explanation, and none was needed. The knife went in between his ribs and I could do nothing to stop it. It seemed to pierce some closed space inside me and leave me as helpless as they left him, and yet as strangely empowered.

The stranger's body went overboard at midnight. Carelessly tossed into the deep. I wanted so much to sleep, and then to awake with a dawn forgetting of an evil dream. But there was no sleep there at the ship's rails, where the black rage of the winter sea had swallowed up the stranger.

For a long time there was nothing. The emptiness seemed to take over not only the ferry, but the sea across which it sailed and the earth that held that sea in its hollows and the universe that held that earth in orbit. All emptiness. Because the black sea had swallowed the Meaning . . .

❧•❧

Out of the depths of the emptiness I felt the swell beneath the planks of the deck strengthening, until I was swaying and cling-ing to the rails to steady myself. The cold night chill on my skin was turning to a biting wind that insinuated its icy fingers into every vein. But the wind that froze my heart so mercilessly also ripped apart the heavy cloud cover from the January night, and for just a split second the sea was bathed in the light of the moon. I gasped, at the shock of the cold and the glory. The in-finite stillness and power of the silver light shone back to me from the crest of every heaving wave and from the depths of every sinking trough. It was as though the moon itself had been plunged into the black sea and had shattered into countless new sources of its own mysterious presence. It was in that terrible plunge into silence that I heard the stranger's Word again, shaking the whole ferry into resonance:

'Give them my love . . . !'

❧•❧

The next morning at breakfast it was almost as though nothing had happened. Most of the passengers had passed the night – sleeping or restless, reeling or sober – without ever encounter-ing the stranger. But here and there, among the travellers, you could see a face that was flickering with something that reminded me strangely of the moonlight.

A family with a baby and a small child sat quietly eating their toast. A peacefulness seemed to radiate from them, that touched everyone who was sitting close to them. A girl in jeans and a blue sweater was talking to a group of friends over their coffee. Whatever she had to say, she was holding their interest like a magnet. The joy in her eyes was somehow imprinting itself onto their own eagerly attentive faces. A lorry driver, carrying his overnight bag, with his anorak thrown lightly across his shoulder, made his way calmly to the car deck. He greeted one of the stewards as he went, with a friendly smile. I never knew that you could transplant a smile, but I saw that steward's face come alive, there and then, with a joy you don't often see, and when you do, you never forget.

The captain closed his log and made his way ashore. Another uneventful night crossing. Perhaps the immigration officer had his suspicions that all was not as it seemed. Not just once, but several times he looked into the face of an otherwise

inconspicuous traveller, and thought he saw the face of someone he had once known, but lost touch with. But it was
probably a trick of his imagination. Whatever it was, each such
encounter left him with a deepening feeling of peace, until he
found himself returning their smiles, gratefully and warmly.
When my turn came I gave him my passport and he responded
with that smile that I had first noticed yesterday across the floor
of the passenger lounge – a smile suffused with the light of one
who both seeks and has found his own deepest meaning. And
I knew that the stranger was no stranger any more, and that the
sea had yielded up its treasure.

CROSSROADS

NIGHT WAS FALLING. The mill-wheel was silent. Charlie had gone to bed on a full stomach. His customers lay sleepless. The Pan Piper had moved on, but his footsteps still shone like stardust in the market square. The pumpkin dreamed of the Ball, and waited. The trees of the forest had a new king, and hardly knew what to do with him. The captain of the North Sea ferry wondered briefly about last night's crossing, before turning over and settling down to rest.

The sun was sinking, and two worldweary travellers made the journey from Jerusalem to the village of Emmaus. They talked, as they walked, and they watched as their own shadows lengthened, until the shadows seemed to be as long and as darkly uncertain as the stony road ahead of them. It was an hour of despair. Dimly they heard the sound of footsteps approaching behind them. Eventually a stranger came alongside them, and gently drew them into conversation. For a while they forgot the long shadows and the stony road. 'What are you discussing so solemnly as you walk?' the stranger asked them.

'Haven't you heard about all that has been happening in Jerusalem this week – how the authorities have crucified Jesus of Nazareth, when we were so sure that he was the Messiah, the one who would bring the Kingdom of God to earth?' they asked him, incredulously. Surely the weight of sorrow upon their own hearts must be affecting the whole world?

'Tell me about it,' he replied.

They walked on. Now three. They told him about their dreams and their despair. About everything they had hoped for, and somehow failed to find. Everything they had trusted in, and how their trust had been betrayed. About the hunger in their bodies and their souls, and the aching in their hearts and in their feet. About loneliness. Rejection. Hopelessness. Systems that trapped them into poverty, and fears that made them doubt themselves. They were surprised at all they told the stranger.

Amazed at the difference a loving companion could make to the journey.

They came to a crossroads. The stranger made to walk on, but they begged him to eat with them at the wayside inn, and he agreed. Together they sat down, and he began to retell their stories. He showed them the landmarks of their own lives, and how each successive mile had been leading them to this moment. This moment of the crossroads, where new possibilities might begin, and new choices might lead in new directions.

They shared bread together. They changed from strangers into companions. Loneliness gave way to community. Despair gave birth, like a phoenix, to a new sense of self-worth. They took the bread that the stranger had blessed, and even as they began to eat it, the stranger disappeared. But he had left something real and permanent behind him. He had left them his empowerment. There would be a tomorrow and they would continue their journey.

༺∘༻

Emmaus is only a few miles from Jerusalem. New hope may only be a few miles from the place of despair. But Emmaus, today and in the here and now, is even closer than that ...

In the devastation of post-war France, Abbé Pierre, a priest, a Member of Parliament and a former Resistance worker, shared his presbytery with the homeless and encouraged them to recycle and sell things that others threw away. It was the first Emmaus community. Abbé Pierre used this name as a sign of the possibility of new hope, new companionship, and the possibility of new directions opening up from crossroads of despair and dereliction.

From that first beginning, there are now over 400 self-supporting Emmaus communities in 44 countries worldwide. Since 1990 the movement has been active in the United Kingdom, where there are seven communities, and a further seventeen are being planned.

This is how the Emmaus movement describes itself.

Emmaus is a secular organisation, inspired by the Christian vision symbolised in the Emmaus journey. It offers homeless people a totally practical way in which they can move from homelessness and dependency on state benefits, to taking responsibility for their own lives by living and working in small self-supporting Communities which aim to provide a family environment.

The residents of such a Community – called Companions – have their own room and share in the responsibility for the Community and for the business as part of a team. All Companions work a full week and share duties according to ability and skill. Everyone is encouraged to develop existing skills and acquire new ones, and various levels of training are provided.

For those without home and livelihood Emmaus offers a real way out of the loneliness and despair, the rejection, fear and isolation of living rough on the streets. Homelessness deprives people of the basic dignity of feeling they matter as real people, with a part to play in the life of a community. Emmaus seeks to restore this dignity in ways that benefit all.

Joining an Emmaus Community is a beginning, not an end. By living and working in Emmaus, people recover their self-respect, discovering for themselves how to take responsibility for their own lives, as well as helping others less fortunate than themselves. Emmaus Communities are committed to active solidarity with those who are marginalised by poverty. Companions use the surplus profits generated by their hard work to help others in need, for example by supporting the local night shelter or providing furniture for those who cannot afford to pay for it.

Above all, Emmaus is a way out of the humiliation of homelessness; a way that offers hope, care and a future.

*This book is dedicated to
the Companions of Emmaus UK.*

It is also a call, to all who pray, to reflect on real and practical ways of turning their contemplation into action.

If you would like to know more about the work of Emmaus, please contact:

Emmaus UK
48 Kingston Street
Cambridge CB1 2NU

Tel: 01223 576103
Fax: 01223 576203
E-mail: emmaus-uk@dial.pipex.com
Web site: http://www.emmaus.org.uk